TO FEEL THIS MUCH

Published by Sungold Editions
Santa Barbara, California

Cover by Gay Phinny
Author photo: Mary Haskell

ISBN-13: 979-8-9867290-2-2

TO FEEL THIS MUCH

POEMS BY

GAY PHINNY

SUNGOLD EDITIONS • 2022

For Wills

With thanks to Laure-Anne Bosselaar, Peter Phinny,
Chryss Yost, Jana Triska, Mary Haskell,
Audrey Evens, Shirley Evens, and Grace.

CONTENTS

I

II

III

I

TWO PEARS

winter melts — snow gives way to green,
shadows grow — together

white light on the inside,
speckled on the outside, like birds' eggs

they are a pair — resting on a weathered
wooden table soaked with years of light.

SUMMER

Inside

    Warm orange light
    glistens like lake water
    on the red Formica table top.

Outside

    soggy marsh, wetlands, green turtle pond
    cat tails, milkweed, Queen Ann's lace
    red-winged blackbirds, purple martins, starlings.

In the sky

    a symphony iridescent,
    dull, scarlet yellow
    glossy black plumage
    forked tails, square tails, fan tails.

Beyond

      notes of color sounds of shapes

      triangle wings, rounded wings, blunt wings

      diving soaring rapid wing beats

      then — glide

Soon,

      fireflies will gather for twilight

      like a string of lights in the sky

      floating, flickering bulbs

      about to burn out.

BEACH

beach-
blue dog
grey gull
sand crabs
big brown ball
animals in the surf
crunchy crustaceans
for the penguins dressed
in their formal, ball wear!

PLAYFUL

Puffins puff
Jellyfish in the sea
Salt on your lips
Jell-O in the bowl
Picnic

&

Owls hoot
Chickadees chick
Bluebirds blow blues
Mockingbirds make mockery
Canaries get out of jail

&

Crows crow
Songbirds sing
Hummingbirds hummmm

I wonder...

      How do sandpipers pipe ?

THE KNOT AROUND MY BREATH

I am a passenger, stuck
in traffic. Red, green, yellow,
                red, green, red.

I look to the left,
                to the right. I see her
— a woman. A dirty yellow letter
sweater binds her breasts.

        Down her white porcelain legs —
blood. She dances by the exit ramp,
                Waves a sign — HELP.

I turn on the radio: classic rock.

PLAYING CATCH

Behind you at a red light
stuck in a traffic jam. Stopped.

Your foot on the brake. Lights.
                    Through your rear window
I watch you sling

something, hurl it, toss it —

a ball? A rag doll? No —
it is screaming. Two of you

are playing catch —
            with a *baby?*

The light turns green, I watch your large hands
            grab the steering wheel,
                        yank it to the right.
The marine layer sinks in. Gray. Cold.

MOON SOUNDS—SKY SOUNDS

Sickle shaped moon.

Stars blink.

The sky lit up
like an operator's board
lights up with calls—

what do they talk about?

SHUTTERED

In a house surrounded by snow
The ring tone of the telephone —
Echoes — bounces off the walls
Then stops.
The handset dead in its cradle.
The kitchen is drenched in blue winter light
Above it, shuttered, the empty nursery.
The floral fabric covered chair
Now occupied by our black cat — curled up.

FUGITIVE

The hands on the face of the clock
wave as they swing past one another.

       Sometimes, they shake hands

or ring a bell.
And sometimes — time stops.

I READ TO HER SOMETIMES

The outlet peers out
from behind the chair:
two electric eyes —
the small O of a mouth.

The upper face is obstructed
by a plug. A cord leads to a lamp
on the table. Some nights
I sit in that chair by that table —
and read to her.

THE WASHING MACHINE

the washing machine turns round and round and round and round
our clothes together — spinning, washing, drying.
Round & round & round
your small shirts, little socks .
I still smell you — imagine your shirt twisted into a braid with mine.
To the left it turns — to the right
swish swish suck gurgle gurgle, drain — the water hums & chortles
again — swish swash, drain, sucking the clothes dry.

What words did we twist?

SHEPHERD DREAMS

Resting next to her ear,
An ancient, bleached
bone she can no longer
see.

Can she hear the ebbing tide,
I wonder? The waves
crashing below?

It is her birthday.

It is dusk.

CIGARETTE AFTER SEX

You have left. The fragrance of you
slides, glides, tiptoes through the room —

twisted velvet glove left on the bedside table
an unlit cigarette — the sheets warm, smooth

and complicated. The sun shimmers —
I'm locked in this moment without you.

INVITATION

Dance across the floor.

                     Move, show me —

so I feel it.

                          Twist, pop, shimmy,

                     bend, crouch —

Skim the floor's luster.

                         Slide —

with the slippery sounds.

                     Push your hair back.

How I remember that:
your fingers parting it.

LEAVING

I was pregnant.

A friend yanked my arm —
leave her.

What I didn't tell M. was,
I had lost my way

I was from the south,
she from the north

In my ear — LOUD —
her whispers lingered

The landscape screamed —
my voice, dirt dry

The child stirred inside me

Silence is where I cry —
When will it scream?

TO FEEL THIS MUCH

The coyote plays —

and is friendly with its prey. Lures it in

to be devoured.

In ice blinding light, they rip —

tear, reach into the warm flesh.

Everyone must eat.

The hare, stripped bare

lays there, cold — yearning,

longing for the end.

To feel this much.

FALL

Scent of shaggy bark eucalyptus.
The lingering onion-like odor of crocus bulbs —
cool hyacinth's blue light.

An earth worm twists, twirls, curls
stretches, digs and
              vanishes/
                  disappears into
black wet watered dirt.

Dogs — haunting howls
                in the distance.

HER AFTERNOON WALK

Mud covered/
cracked leather/

brown boots
a pair

back door —
WAIT

EVERYWHERE

the stars blink away — poof! —

and disappear

a warm sun slowly rises

from the east

orb of orange

the stars now rest

until the next time

though we think they have vanished — they have not

like   Love

they are everywhere

IMMIGRANTS

Inside the wall's shivering
shadows, looking up
huddled, coiled souls
like barbed wire.
the clatter of helicopters
like bullets overhead
rotor blades
like knives.

THE ROPE

When it snows and snows and snows
that heaviness, and cold
stare me in the heart, oppressive.
Ice slides off the roof, breaks —
crashes to the ground.

Nothing can lift this heaviness,
barely breathing. The bleak
wild swirls circle — the view
nonexistent from here, a white out
is what they say.

Around here people tie a rope
from their house to their barn
so that they don't get lost
after feeding the horses.

THIRSTY

I walk

     and walk

          and walk

I am thirsty —

I can hear the river.

TELL HER THE ANGEL IS BLUE

Tell her the angel is blue.
    That the lake is deep. I have
        been in this landscape before

of raw umber grey. I quieted my voice — too
    strong: my throat choked with brown dirt.
        My truth was not welcomed by the white haired man.

Like hoarfrost, I felt cold inside — naked, peeled stark.

Why is my voice too loud? No one ever told me.
    They snapped, *shush!* Like lightening: a sudden
        crack without warning. Until one day

it becomes who I am: a part of me. And this is
    not my truth.

I search and search. Listen and listen. Hear and hear.
    I look and look. The mystery lives in me. Do angels
        sing the loudest before the deepest silence?

EARLY MORNING

The din of traffic
the distant dove attempts to be
louder — her voice is barely audible
yet crystal clear

like God's.

GRACE

I am following the moon in my living room
through the octagonal sky light

she moves, I move —
the chair that holds me becomes heavy to lift

so I slide it across the wooden floor
— the moon is now veiled in a marine layer

night sky — so beautiful —
Grace?

She sits just behind the old eucalyptus
just out of reach.

When can I touch you?
And you, me ?

ABOUT THE POET

Phinny is an avid hiker, bird watcher, and animal lover who currently lives in Santa Monica, California. Much of her writing is inspired by her early morning walks on the beach, in the canyons, and the Santa Monica mountains.